HO CHI MINH

PHILIP STEELE

Heinemann LIBRARY

H www.heinemann.co.uk/library
Visit our website to find out more information about **Heinemann Library** books.

To order:
☎ Phone 44 (0) 1865 888066
▤ Send a fax to 44 (0) 1865 314091
▢ Visit the Heinemann Bookshop at www.heinemann.co.uk/library to browse our catalogue and order online.

First published in Great Britain by Heinemann Library, Halley Court, Jordan Hill, Oxford OX2 8EJ, part of Harcourt Education.

Heinemann is a registered trademark of Harcourt Education Ltd.

Produced for Heinemann by Discovery Books Ltd
Editorial: Helen Dwyer, Nicole Irving, Andrew Solway and Jennifer Tubbs
Design: Barry Dwyer
Illustrations: Stefan Chabluk
Picture research: Rachel Tisdale
Production: Séverine Ribierre

Originated by Dot Gradations
Printed and bound in China by South China Printing Company

ISBN 0 431 13878 8
07 06 05 04 03
10 9 8 7 6 5 4 3 2 1

British Library Cataloguing in Publication Data
Steele, Philip
  Ho Chi Minh. – (Leading lives)
  959.7'043'092

A full catalogue record for this book is available from the British Library.

Acknowledgements
The publishers would like to thank the following for permission to reproduce photographs: Camera Press: pp. **18, 37, 39, 47**; Corbis: pp. **7** (Tim Page), **9** (Archivo Iconografico, S.A.), **10** (Steve Raymer), **12, 22** (Hulton Deutsch Collection), **25, 40, 43, 54** (Bettmann), **50, 52** (Steve Raymer), **55** (Macduff Everton); Hulton Archive: pp. **20, 27, 32, 35, 49**; Peter Newark: pp. **26, 28**; Popperfoto: pp. **4, 15, 41, 45**.

Cover photograph of Ho Chi Minh reproduced with permission of Hulton Archive.

Every effort has been made to contact copyright holders of any material reproduced in this book. Any omissions will be rectified in subsequent printings if notice is given to the publishers.

Contents

1 For Vietnam!   4

2 The flier of kites   6

   Map of Indochina c.1890   6

3 'One who will succeed'   9

4 Citizen of the world   11

5 The Red Flag   16

6 The secret agent   20

7 Troubled times   23

8 The world at war   28

   Map of China and South-east Asia, 1931–41   30

9 The Vietminh   31

10 Return of the French   35

11 A land divided   40

12 The Vietnam War   44

13 An old man dies   48

14 The world after Ho   51

Timeline   56

Key people of Ho Chi Minh's time   58

Further reading and other resources   60

Glossary   61

Index   64

Any words appearing in the text in bold, **like this**, are explained in the Glossary.

It was 2 September 1945. All morning, thousands of people, young and old, had poured into the city of Hanoi, in Vietnam. Merchants were shutting up their shops and joining the excited crowds in the square. People were carrying flowers and there were red flags and banners on every street.

A call for freedom

Shortly after 2 o'clock a thin, simply-dressed man climbed up on to the public platform. He looked out over the sea of faces, the young men in white shirts, many village women in colourful robes. Some of the old men were holding ancient weapons from past wars.

The man on the platform was Ho Chi Minh, Vietnam's new leader. He declared that his country would no longer be ruled by the French or the Japanese. Long ago, he said, the French people had risen up against an unjust king, and people in the USA had rebelled against the rule of the British. They had declared that all men were born free and had equal rights. Vietnam too would now become an independent nation.

As Ho Chi Minh finished speaking and stepped down, he must have been looking back over his life and his long struggle to make this dream come true. He knew only too well that the struggle was far from over.

A man of his times

'Who is this man?' muttered some people in the crowd, as the cheers died down. It was a good question. Ho Chi Minh was not well

◀ Ho Chi Minh spent all his adult life fighting for an independent, united, Communist state of Vietnam.

known to the people of Hanoi. For many years, he had led a secret life. He had changed his name several times and had lived in many different parts of the world.

During the next 20 years, however, the name of Ho Chi Minh became famous not just in South-east Asia, but around the world.

Ho Chi Minh lived in stormy times. When he was born in 1890, powerful European countries were extending their rule over most of the world. The struggle of those lands to regain their freedom would last all his lifetime.

In the early 20th century political systems that had been in place for hundreds of years were coming under attack. The Chinese emperor was forced from power in 1911, the Russian emperor in 1917. Inspired by the Russian **revolution**, **Communists** were calling for workers all over the world to seize power. Severe economic problems in the 1920s and 1930s allowed **dictators** to take over Italy, Germany and Spain.

Ho Chi Minh's life coincided with conflict on a global scale. Between 1914 and 1918 the great powers of the day turned on each other in World War One, with loss of life on a vast scale. From 1939 to 1945 there was a second World War, which was followed by the **Cold War** (1945–90), a long period of tension between the USA and the Soviet Union. Ho Chi Minh was witness to and involved in many events which shaped world history.

The flier of kites

Vietnam is a country in South-east Asia, to the east of Laos and Cambodia. It is mountainous in the northwest, but in the east a hot, humid plain borders the blue waters of the South China Sea. Much of the land is covered in tropical forests and rice fields. Most Vietnamese people live around the Hong River, in the north, and the Mekong River in the south.

Village boy

The man we know as 'Ho Chi Minh' was born with the name Nguyen Sinh Cung, on 19 May 1890. His birthplace was the village of Hoang Tru, near the city of Vinh. Although Vietnam still had its own emperor at that time, it was governed by France as part of a territory called Indochina.

As a little boy, Ho Chi Minh liked to play with his elder brother and sister, running along the paths flying his paper kite. His mother, Hoang Thi Loan, enjoyed singing and telling tales to her children.

Sadness in the city

When the boy was five, his family moved south to the city of Hué, where his father,

◀ This map shows Vietnam as it was in 1890. There were three regions called Tonkin, Annam and Cochin China. Together with Laos and Cambodia they formed French-ruled Indochina.

▲ *Ho Chi Minh lived in this house in the village of Kim Lien after his mother's death in 1901.*

Nguyen Sinh Sac, was to study. Sadly, his mother died there while giving birth to another baby in 1901. Ho and the other children had to return to Hoang Tru, where they were cared for by their grandmother until their father passed his exams.

When Nguyen Sinh Sac returned north, he was expected to take a job at the emperor's court, but he refused, saying that he was too upset by his wife's death. Instead he set up a little school in his home village of Kim Lien. He was a clever man, widely respected for his learning.

New ideas

There was another reason for Nguyen Sinh Sac to refuse the job. Like many of his friends, he had no time for the royal court, which under French rule no longer had any real power. He was a **nationalist**, who opposed French rule,

Key dates: Vietnam in the 19th century

1802	• Vietnam united as a single empire
1859	• French capture the southern city of Saigon
1862	• French gain control of central Vietnam (known as Annam)
1867	• French gain control of south Vietnam (which they call Cochin China)
1874	• French invade north Vietnam (known as Tonkin)
1885	• All Vietnam comes under French control
1887	• Laos, Cambodia and Vietnam are united under French rule as Indochina

believing that his country had the right to rule itself. He also refused to speak the French language, which was necessary for anyone wishing to take up an official job at this time. Interested in Vietnamese history and writing, he also wanted to learn more about European and American ideas and the modern world. Young Ho Chi Minh loved to hear his father arguing about politics and ideas and soon showed that he was quick to learn.

3 'One who will succeed'

It was an old Vietnamese custom that boys were given a new name when they were no longer infants, as a sign that they were growing up. Aged 11, Ho Chi Minh was now given the name Nguyen Tat Thanh, which means 'one who will succeed'.

Teachers and lessons

Most teachers at that time expected children to learn their lessons off by heart. But Ho Chi Minh was taught for a time by his father and by a family friend called Vuong Thuc Qui, a **nationalist** rebel. They disliked parrot-style learning and instead taught young Ho Chi Minh to think for himself.

One of Ho Chi Minh's favourite books as a boy was an old Chinese story called *Journey to the West*, full of monsters, demons and the fantastic adventures of a character called 'Monkey'.

In 1905, aged 15, Ho Chi Minh was sent to a school in Vinh, where he learned to speak French. Even nationalists agreed that the French would never be defeated if the Vietnamese could not understand their language.

The student rebel

The following year, Nguyen Sinh Sac was again asked to work for the royal court as an official. He could not refuse this time without being marked out as a rebel, so he travelled back to Hué with a heavy heart.

▶ *As a child Ho studied the ideas of the Chinese **philosopher** Confucius (551–479 BCE). China had ruled Vietnam in ancient times, and the teachings of Confucius were still believed to be very important.*

In 1907 Ho Chi Minh passed the entrance exam for the National Academy in Hué. Some rich students made fun of Ho Chi Minh for being a poor country boy. He took no notice and studied hard, learning science and geography.

Life was very hard for the country people in Indochina at this time. In 1908, poor villagers poured into Hué from the countryside, protesting against taxes. Ho Chi Minh went out to join them and offered to translate their demands to the authorities into French. The protestors were ordered to go away and when they refused were fired upon by French troops. The next day, Ho Chi Minh was expelled from the National Academy.

Heading south

It was the beginning of hard times for all Ho's family, who were persecuted by the imperial security forces. Ho's father was moved to a job in a region 300 kilometres from Hué.

Ho Chi Minh himself went into hiding and then travelled south, working for a time as a teacher. In 1911 he ended up in the great city of Saigon and began to dream of leaving his homeland to find out more about the world.

◀ *Today, farmland still stretches beyond the old city walls of Hué, where peasants protested in 1908.*

4 Citizen of the world

It was June 1911 when 21-year-old Ho Chi Minh boarded a French steamer anchored in Saigon. The young man had registered under a false name, Van Ba. He was not to be a passenger, but a worker. The ship was about to sail to France and back.

TO LOCATE SAIGON, SEE THE MAP ON PAGE 6.

On leaving home
'I saw that I must go abroad to see for myself. After I had found out how they lived, I would return ... to help my countrymen.'
(Ho Chi Minh)

To France and back
Ho Chi Minh toiled all hours of the day and night, scrubbing down the decks and fetching and carrying sacks of food for the cook. The seas were rough in the Indian Ocean and the ship pitched and tossed. At last it passed through the Suez Canal into the Mediterranean Sea and finally docked at Marseille, in the south of France.

Ho Chi Minh's first impressions of Europe were mixed. He was surprised to discover how many French people were poor, too. He also found that some were friendly towards him. Ho's ship then sailed north to Le Havre, before the return voyage to Vietnam.

The wanderer
Ho Chi Minh did not stay long in Saigon. He began a period of wandering around the world, working his passage on ships and taking all kinds of jobs on shore.

He went back to France and then to the seaports of North and West Africa, Arabia, India and Madagascar. Wherever he travelled, he was horrified by the poverty of local people and the harshness of European colonial rule. Local people had no political rights and could not vote. Imprisonment was common and punishments were often brutal. Employment was often little better than slavery, with terrible working conditions and little reward.

Ho Chi Minh also visited South America and in 1913 spent some time in the United States. He found odd jobs in New York City and Boston. He was astounded by the skyscrapers and modern technology, but saddened by the way in which the whites treated the African Americans he met there.

▼ *New York City in 1910. The city made a lasting impression on Ho Chi Minh in 1913. In the USA, he worked as a labourer and as a servant.*

Soon Ho Chi Minh was in England. He worked in two well-known hotels in London, learning to be an assistant pastry chef. He was shocked by the amount of food wasted in the hotels, at a time when poor people were going hungry.

War years

The Great War – which we now call World War One – broke out in August 1914. Ho Chi Minh soon realized that this would be war on a scale the world had never known before. The rulers of the world's biggest overseas empires – Great Britain, France, Germany and Belgium – seemed to be locked into a fight to the bitter end. Surely this would also bring an end to their power? Perhaps the peoples they ruled would not have to fight for their freedom after all?

In 1917 Ho Chi Minh crossed the English Channel and settled in Paris. He found work as a photo retoucher – in the days before colour photography, people liked to have their black-and-white pictures tinted by hand. In his spare time, he studied in libraries and improved his understanding of French.

Ho Chi Minh found that many other young Vietnamese were now living in France. They had been brought over from the **colonies** to work in the factories, because so many Frenchmen were away fighting in the war. With them, he discussed the future of his homeland and ways in which its people could become free.

The idealist

Ho Chi Minh read all the books he could find about the American and French **revolutions** that had taken place over 200 years before. He was inspired by the **revolutionaries**, by their belief that all humans are born equal, by their shared ideals of freedom, justice and the brotherhood of all peoples.

Ho Chi Minh's travels had interested him in **social justice** and **human rights**, not just in Vietnam but around the world. He and his friends discussed the situation in China, where the **nationalist** Sun Zhongshan (sometimes called Sun Yat-sen) had overthrown the emperor in 1911, and in Russia, where a **Communist** revolution took place in November 1917.

The world seemed to be changing very rapidly. However, when the war came to an end in 1918, the European empires were still in place and seemed to be as powerful as ever.

Demands for change

In 1919, Ho Chi Minh and his friends set up a society called the Association of Annamese (that is, Vietnamese) **Patriots**. The Patriots drew up a list of demands for **democratic** reform. Ho Chi Minh signed the document 'Nguyen Ai Quoc'. He used this false name for many years to avoid detection by his enemies.

The leaders of Europe and the USA were gathering at this time in Versailles, near Paris, to draw up an international

Demands of the Patriots

- pardons and release for people imprisoned for their political views in Vietnam
- equal rights for all citizens
- freedom for newspapers, magazines, and radio to express their views; freedom to hold meetings and organize political groups and trade unions to protect workers' pay and working conditions
- freedom to travel abroad
- a proper education system
- government by rule of law – elected representatives being sent to the French parliament.

▲ *The world's leading powers met at Versailles in 1919 to plan the new world order.*

peace treaty. Ho Chi Minh and his friends decided that this was a good time to **lobby** governments about the future of their country. They published their demands in the press and handed them in to members of the French parliament (the National Assembly) and to the French president himself.

They also gave their demands to the foreign politicians meeting at Versailles. Ho Chi Minh especially hoped that the United States would be sympathetic, as American governments had often criticized the European-ruled empires. Surely the demands that he and his friends were making were just the same as the ones being put forward at the peace conference?

No reply

It seemed that the ideals of the USA and European nations did not apply to the peoples they ruled in distant parts of the world. The American government thanked Ho Chi Minh for the document, but took no action. The French were angered by the demands. They immediately set secret police agents on the trail of this 'Nguyen Ai Quoc'. But copies of the document arrived in Vietnam and were passed around among nationalist supporters there.

The Red Flag

At the age of 30, Ho Chi Minh was a good-looking man, with glossy black hair and bright, intelligent eyes. It was now December 1920 and, dressed in a smart suit and tie, he was travelling to the French city of Tours, where there was to be a big conference of French **socialists**.

Ho Chi Minh had met many socialists since his return to France in 1917. These people hoped to create a new kind of society, run by the working people rather than the **capitalists** (the people who grew rich by owning companies or by buying and selling **shares**).

Which way forward?

Some socialists believed that the best way to bring about their ideal world was to take part in the existing political system and call for reform or gradual change. Others declared that real change could only happen if workers all over the world rose up and seized power for themselves. This was the only way in which the whole economic and political system would be completely changed, they said. This was how to create a fair society.

FOR DETAILS ON KEY PEOPLE OF HO CHI MINH'S TIME, SEE PAGE 58.

Ho Chi Minh became very interested in the ideas being discussed. He read the books of the German political thinker Karl Marx (1818–83) and of Vladimir Ilyich Lenin, the **Communist** who had led the **revolution** in Russia in November 1917. He came to agree that a revolution was needed, and believed that only this would bring real freedom for the people of Vietnam.

Talking in Tours

Ho Chi Minh arrived in Tours, followed by the French government's secret agents, who were always on his tail. At the conference, he made quite an impression. Ho Chi Minh declared that the struggle for freedom in lands such as Vietnam should be at the centre of any socialist policy.

Many of the people there disagreed. They believed that the revolution would not be brought about by farmers growing rice in the villages of Asia, but by workers in the factories, mines and steel mills of Europe and America.

At the end of the meeeting in Tours, Ho Chi Minh voted for the founding of a new French Communist Party, which would be part of the Communist International (known as the '**Comintern**'). This alliance had been set up in Moscow in March 1919, with the aim of bringing together all the different Communist parties around the world.

Ho Chi Minh continued with his political **campaigns**, writing articles and building up links with people from other **colonies**. He often had fierce arguments with other socialists. He was poor, but still found time to enjoy himself in Paris, making many friends and visiting museums and galleries.

The land of revolution
In 1923, Ho Chi Minh sailed to Russia, which had just renamed itself the Union of Soviet Socialist Republics, or 'Soviet Union'. He was invited to Russia by the Comintern, which wanted to hear his views.

The Soviet Union was a whirlwind of activity and argument. These were exciting times, but everyday life was chaotic. Even Ho Chi Minh was **detained** for weeks before he was given official permission to enter the country.

Moscow life

FOR DETAILS ON KEY PEOPLE OF HO CHI MINH'S TIME, SEE PAGE 58.

At last he settled in Moscow and was given work with the Far Eastern office of the Comintern, which was setting up contacts with Communists in China and South-east Asia. He also studied at university, where he met many people who would play an important part in history. Jiang Jieshi (Chiang Kai-Shek) was one of them. He was a Chinese **nationalist** and a brilliant soldier who ended up as president of the Chinese republic. He proved to be extremely hostile to the Chinese Communists, but in the 1930s he was forced to fight alongside them against a Japanese invasion.

◀ *The Chinese nationalist leader Sun Zhongshang (or Sun Yat-sen) is shown here in 1923 with Jiang Jieshi (left), whom Ho Chi Minh met in Moscow.*

Ho also met Zhou Enlai (Chou En-Lai). This leading member of the Chinese Communist Party helped to bring about a Communist victory in China and served as Prime Minister from 1949 to 1975. In January 1924, Ho Chi Minh was greatly saddened by the death of the Soviet leader, Lenin.

Ho Chi Minh found himself having the same arguments in Moscow that he had in France. Many of his fellow Communists would not agree that freedom for people living in colonies such as Vietnam was an urgent part of the revolution. Some saw it as a side issue or as a later stage.

Marx and Lenin had said that a just society would only be created once the **working classes** in all countries were free. True national freedom would only come from international struggle. Ho Chi Minh agreed, but the injustices of his childhood in Vietnam were fresh in his mind. He could tell of overcrowded jails, of toil in the rubber **plantations**, of the way in which Europeans despised his people. To him, freedom for Vietnam and all the other European colonies was not only a just cause but a key part of any revolution.

The colonies count!

*'Why do you neglect the **colonies**, while **capitalism** uses them to support itself, defend itself and fight you?'*
(Ho Chi Minh, in an address to the 5th Congress of the Comintern, 1924)

Ho Chi Minh longed to be back in his own part of the world. Since signing the list of demands drawn up by Vietnamese nationalists in Versailles he could not return to Vietnam without being arrested by the French, but revolution was in the air in neighbouring China and he wanted to be part of it.

The secret agent

In October 1924 Ho Chi Minh was sent by the **Comintern** on a secret mission – to make contact with **revolutionaries** in the east. The train steamed out of Moscow and crossed the Ural Mountains into the vast eastern wilderness of Siberia. For day after day the train steamed through forests of birch and spruce and rattled through villages of wooden houses.

Even today a journey on the Trans-Siberian railway can take a week. Then, it took three times as long. Mounted soldiers of the Red (Soviet) Army patrolled the line and checked travel permits. At last the train steamed into Vladivostok, the Soviet Union's chief port on the Pacific coast.

To Guangzhou

From there Ho Chi Minh took a ship southwards, following the coast of China. It docked amid the hooting steamships and wooden sailing vessels in the busiest harbour in southern China. The foreign traders based there called this great city Canton, but its Chinese name was Guangzhou.

In the early 1920s, much of China was in a state of chaos. The Chinese **nationalists** who had seized power in 1911 had not

▼ A gun-boat patrols Guangzhou harbour. The 1920s were troubled times in China.

been able to keep control of the whole country. Regional **warlords** had seized power. In their efforts to rule all China, the nationalists were now in alliance with the newly formed Chinese **Communist** Party. Guangzhou was then the chief city of this alliance and Ho Chi Minh was keen to make contact with people from both sides.

The port of Guangzhou lay just across the sea from Vietnam and Ho Chi Minh found many other Vietnamese **exiles** in town. They had very different political plans for their homeland. Some were nationalists and others were Communists. Some were planning acts of terrorism.

To LOCATE GUANGZHOU, SEE THE MAP ON PAGE 30.

Ho Chi Minh spread among them the ideas of Marx and Lenin and built up support for the Comintern. He also put these ideas into a weekly newspaper which was sent over to Vietnam, where anti-French feelings were growing every day.

Ho Chi Minh's time in Guangzhou was not just given over to politics. He got married at this time, too, to a beautiful young woman called Tang Tuyet Minh. They liked each other well enough, but they had little in common. It soon became clear that the marriage was a mistake. She thought he was a bit too old for her and he could not interest her in his political dreams.

On the run

The alliance between the Chinese nationalists and Communists had never been very strong and it was soon over. Sun Zhongshan had died and the new leader of the nationalists was Jiang Jieshi, whom Ho Chi Minh had met in Moscow. In March 1927, in the Chinese city of Shanghai, Jiang Jieshi ordered the killing of about 5,000 Communists and also of any nationalists who disagreed with him.

Guangzhou was next on Jiang Jieshi's list and the Communists in that city knew that their time was up. By May 1927, Ho Chi Minh had to leave his new wife behind and flee the city for Hong Kong, a small territory on the southern coast of China which was at that time a British **colony**. Although Ho wrote letters to his wife they never lived together again.

In the months that followed, Ho Chi Minh travelled around the world as an agent for the Comintern. He went back to Moscow, to Germany, France, Italy, then by ship to Siam (today known as Thailand). He used different names, wore disguises and travelled on false papers. He was a wanted man, with the police normally only one step behind him. It was a desperate way of life and he was often short of money and food.

However Ho Chi Minh was sure that it was all worthwhile. **Communism** was on the rise and **capitalism** seemed to be failing – just as Marx and Lenin had said it would. Even in London, at the heart of the powerful British Empire, **striking** workers were battling with the government. And in 1929 the economy of the USA collapsed overnight, starting a period called the **Great Depression**. It affected the whole world. If the European powers had not been destroyed by World War One, surely failings in their own economic system would prove to be their downfall?

◀ It is 1927 and military police in Shanghai arrest a suspected Communist.

7 **Troubled times**

Many people were now working to end French rule in Vietnam, both inside and outside the country. Vietnamese **nationalists** had founded a new movement called the Viet Quoc in 1927. They wished to create a new **capitalist** state in Vietnam. The **Communists** too were gaining new recruits. Indeed, several different groups had grown up. They included an Annam Communist Party, an Indochinese Communist League and a Communist Party of Indochina.

Each had its own views on the way forward. How should they be allied to the Chinese Communist Party? Should they be starting a **revolution** in Vietnam at this point, or be building up support for later? Various groups were trying to recruit each other's members and there was rivalry between the north and the south, too.

A new Communist party

Only one person was able to sort out the confusion – Ho Chi Minh. He could not re-enter French Indochina, where he was a wanted man with a price on his head. Instead, he travelled from Siam to Hong Kong. It had replaced Guangzhou as the chief centre for Vietnamese **exiles** and **revolutionaries**.

Ho Chi Minh was always good at dealing with people and getting them to work together. In Hong Kong he calmed down hurt feelings and looked for common ground between representatives from the different Vietnamese groups. Together in February 1930 they agreed to form a united Vietnamese Communist Party.

Later that year, word came from the **Comintern** in Moscow that the name of the party should be changed to the 'Indochinese Communist Party'. The name was meant to reflect the region as a whole and to make it clear that Vietnamese independence was not the first aim of the party. This change showed up a lasting difference of opinion between Ho Chi Minh and Moscow.

Storms in Vietnam

In Vietnam itself, the **Great Depression** was having its effect. French businesses were in trouble and were pulling out money from their **plantations**, mines and factories. There was a lot of hardship.

In the years 1931 and 1932 there were violent uprisings by both nationalists and Communists. Ho Chi Minh was pleased to see the French government in trouble in Vietnam, but was worried that the time was not yet right for a full **revolution**. He called for caution.

A Hong Kong prison

During the 1930s, police in all the **colonies** of Asia were looking out for troublemakers. Many rebels were being arrested in Vietnam. On 6 June 1931 the Hong Kong police pulled in Ho Chi Minh, who, at the time, was claiming to be a Chinese citizen.

The British authorities held him in prison, but found difficulty in proving any charges against him. Jail was unpleasant and

A most accomplished man

'A most accomplished man, speaking half-a-dozen European langages ... a firm believer ... that the pen is mightier than the sword.'

(Press report at the time of Ho Chi Minh's arrest in Hong Kong)

24

the food was poor. Ho Chi Minh became ill. This was a low point in his life. Many of his personal and political friends were also being arrested. These included a new love in his life, another Vietnamese Communist whose name was Nguyen Thi Minh Kai. She was a leading **campaigner** for women's rights. After their affair ended Nguyen Thi Minh Kai went to Moscow in 1934 and there married another leading Vietnamese Communist.

The British authorities wanted to **deport** Ho Chi Minh. After many arguments in courts, in both Hong Kong and Great Britain, he was finally released in December 1932. Photographs of him at this time show a thin, worried-looking man whose hard life was beginning to show in his face. And more troubles lay ahead.

Stalin's terror

Ho Chi Minh now travelled to Shanghai and then back across Siberia to Moscow, where he arrived in 1934. He found that the Soviet Union had changed greatly under the leadership of Joseph Stalin. Many of the original Russian revolutionaries had been put on trial and imprisoned. Stalin's chief opponent, Leon Trotsky, had been sent into exile in 1929. From 1928 Stalin had imposed agricultural reform in the face of determined opposition by the kulaks (peasants who owned land). He was brutal in his opposition to them and many were executed.

▲ In the 1920s and 1930s Ho Chi Minh was forever on the move, changing identity, in and out of prison.

FOR DETAILS ON KEY PEOPLE OF HO CHI MINH'S TIME, SEE PAGE 58.

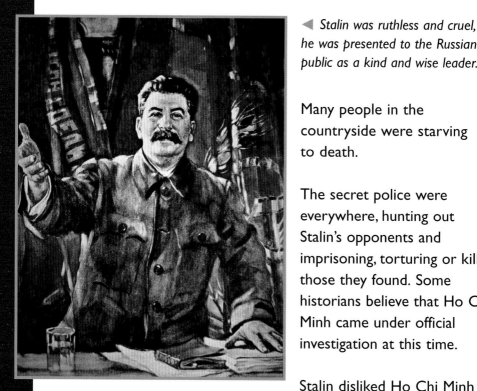

Stalin was ruthless and cruel, but he was presented to the Russian public as a kind and wise leader.

Many people in the countryside were starving to death.

The secret police were everywhere, hunting out Stalin's opponents and imprisoning, torturing or killing those they found. Some historians believe that Ho Chi Minh came under official investigation at this time.

Stalin disliked Ho Chi Minh personally, but still needed him in South-east Asia as a future Soviet ally. Ho Chi Minh in turn needed Soviet support for his struggle to liberate Vietnam. At that point, there was no other country prepared or able to help.

While in the Soviet Union, Ho Chi Minh publicly claimed to support Stalin. He probably had little choice. If he had spoken out against Stalin's policies, he would certainly have been in deep trouble. In private, he must have been very worried about what he saw going on in the Soviet Union.

Another way?

Was there no other way forward for Ho Chi Minh? In the 1930s another great colonial struggle was going on in India. Its leader, an Indian called Mohandas Karamchand Gandhi, was

campaigning for freedom from British rule. Like Ho Chi Minh, Gandhi admired the traditional values of the farmers and villagers in his own country. However Gandhi resisted British rule with non-violence rather than revolution.

Ho Chi Minh believed that Gandhi could never bring about lasting social change because his political ideals were not based on hard economic facts but more on **spiritual** values. Ho Chi Minh admired Gandhi greatly as a human being and as someone engaged in the same struggle. However he himself still chose to follow the path of revolution, not reform.

▶ *Both Ho Chi Minh and Gandhi (centre) were struggling to liberate their peoples from rule by powerful empires. Gandhi (1869–1948) became known as 'Mahatma', meaning 'great soul'.*

A disciple

'I and others may be revolutionaries, but we are all disciples of Mahatma Gandhi, nothing more, nothing less.'

(Ho Chi Minh)

The world at war

It was 1938 and Ho Chi Minh was on the move once again, glad to be leaving Moscow. From his train he could see the dusty grasslands and cotton fields of Central Asia flying past the window. The **Comintern** was sending him back to China, but this time he was to travel overland from Kazakhstan, crossing China's western borders and then travelling to the city of Xi'an. From there he headed south, walking, riding on horseback, lurching over rough roads on lorries. The whole country seemed to be on the move. China was at war with Japan.

TO LOCATE XI'AN, SEE THE MAP ON PAGE 30.

The war in China

Japan had occupied the northeast of China back in 1931 and it was now bombing cities and invading the rest of the country. Japanese troops were being resisted by both Chinese **nationalists** and **Communists**. Faced with a common enemy, they had had to join forces once more. Where would the Japanese stop? It seemed that they were not just trying to control China, but the whole of South-east Asia.

Ho Chi Minh travelled under a false name as usual. Everyone assumed he was Chinese. He at last arrived in Guilin, an old city in south-east China, set in beautiful countryside amid lakes, cliffs and pillars of limestone rock. Travelling through this classical Chinese

◄ In July 1937 Japanese troops had captured China's capital city, Beijing.

landscape must have made him think of the adventures he had read about as a boy in *Journey to the West*.

In Guilin Ho Chi Minh worked at the regional headquarters of the United Front (an alliance of Chinese nationalists and Communists), editing their journal and organizing public health. He also wrote articles for a French-language Vietnamese newspaper called *Notre Voix* (Our Voice), filing reports on Japanese **atrocities** in China and on the Chinese resistance. He later made many further travels in China, reporting back to the Comintern in Moscow and making contacts. All the time, he kept in touch with the Communist rebels in Vietnam.

TO LOCATE GUILIN, SEE THE MAP ON PAGE 30.

France and Japan

From China, Ho Chi Minh followed the international news with the greatest interest. In 1939 World War Two broke out in Europe. The murderous **Nazi** government, which had come to power in Germany, was at war with Great Britain and France. At first the Soviet leader, Joseph Stalin, made a deal with the Germans, but by 1941 the Soviet Union too was fighting against the Nazis.

The German invasion of France in 1940 was of great interest to Ho Chi Minh. How would it affect Vietnam? The Germans set up a pro-German French government in the town of Vichy, in France. It was this 'Vichy' government which took control of most of France's **colonies**, although many French people in the colonies fled to set up anti-Vichy groups, fighting as the 'Free French'.

In September 1940 the Vichy government agreed that Japanese troops could march into Vietnam, provided that the French were still allowed to run the country. Many Vietnamese

Key
Japanese gains 1931–37
Japanese gains 1938–41

SOVIET UNION

MONGOLIA

Sea of Japan

JAPAN

KOREA (annexed 1910)

Beijing

Xi'an

Shanghai

CHINA

Guilin

Kunming

INDIA

Guangzhou

Hong Kong

TAIWAN

PACIFIC OCEAN

BURMA

South China Sea

SIAM (THAILAND)

PHILIPPINES

FRENCH INDOCHINA

N
W — E
S

0   500 km

0   500 miles

▲ *During the 1930s and 1940s Japanese troops swept through China and South-east Asia.*

nationalists welcomed the Japanese. They believed that because they were fellow Asians, the Japanese would eventually free them from their European masters.

Ho Chi Minh warned against such ideas. Japanese invasion was not the answer to French rule, he declared, just part of the same problem.

9 The Vietminh

World war made one thing very certain. Now was time for the Vietnamese to start their fight for freedom. In China, Ho Chi Minh and his followers began to set up a new secret force called the Vietminh. It aimed to unite **Communists** and **nationalists** – provided they were prepared to fight both the French and the Japanese.

The new organization was given the official go-ahead at a conference of the Indochinese Communist Party in March 1941. This meeting was held in an extraordinary place – a remote cave in the Pac Bo valley, just inside the Vietnamese border. Ho Chi Minh was there in person, for he had secretly crossed back into his homeland. He was living rough, training new recruits and preparing for war. The Vietminh rebels had to dodge patrols of soldiers and would have been tortured and killed if captured.

TO LOCATE PAC BO, SEE THE MAP ON PAGE 6.

At 50, Ho was not as fit as the young ones, but despite the danger and the hardship, he was in good spirits. He was home again after 30 years. He earned the respect of the rebels and it was during this period that the man of many names was first called 'Ho Chi Minh', which means 'bringer of enlightenment (clarity and reason)'.

In December 1941 Ho Chi Minh and his rebels in their hideout were amazed to hear that Japan had bombed Pearl Harbor, an American naval base in the Pacific. This meant that Japan and the USA were also now at war. Ho Chi Minh ordered the Vietminh operations in the north to be spread to other parts of the country. He also began to wonder if the USA might not end up being a useful ally, now that they had a common enemy.

Chinese prisons

Ho Chi Minh needed international support for the Vietminh. In the summer of 1942 he crossed back into China to seek backing from the Chinese nationalists and Communists. However he was soon arrested by the police, who found he was carrying false identity papers. They thought he must be a secret agent working for the Japanese.

Ho Chi Minh was passed from one jail to another. He was kept in grim conditions and became very sick with **tuberculosis**. It was months before anyone realized who this prisoner really was, and even then the Chinese nationalists were far from eager to allow his release. It was over a year before he was given limited freedom and he did not get back into Vietnam until September 1944.

American allies

In November 1944, an American plane crashed in northern Vietnam and Rudolph Shaw, the pilot who had escaped, was

◄ *Serving with the Vietminh forces in the 1940s and 1950s, Ho Chi Minh became a man of action.*

brought in to Ho Chi Minh's base at Pac Bo. Ho Chi Minh guided him to safety across the Chinese border and went on to Kunming in the south of China.

TO LOCATE KUNMING, SEE THE MAP ON PAGE 30.

This city was the capital of the anti-Japanese alliance in China. The British and Americans were sending supplies and weapons into Kunming at this time and there were American officials and soldiers there. Ho Chi Minh met up with them several times and asked for help in their common fight against the Japanese.

Meeting the Americans

'The old man wears Chinese-type cotton trousers and buttoned-to-the-neck jacket ... His little beard is silvery ... his hair is still almost black. They [Ho and his colleague] both talk quietly but sometimes burst into chuckles. We seem to get on well together.'

(Lt Charles Fenn, US Marines, describing his meeting with Ho Chi Minh in China in 1945)

Some of the Americans were interested in making contact with the Vietminh. They could not give this organization their official backing, for the USA still recognized France's claim to Vietnam. However they did provide a radio operator, medicines and some weapons. They were suspicious of Ho's Communist connections, but could not help but admire this ragged **revolutionary** who had walked in out of nowhere.

While Ho Cho Minh was talking to the Americans in China, World War Two was already drawing to its end. In Europe the Germans had been pushed out of France and Paris itself was now in the hands of the Free French.

The final days

In Vietnam there was a terrible **famine** and the Japanese were seizing all the food supplies they could lay their hands on. They knew they were losing the war. In March 1945 they forced the French from power in Vietnam and handed over government to the Vietnamese emperor, Bao Dai. Though real power was still held by the Japanese, that would not last for long.

FOR DETAILS ON KEY PEOPLE OF HO CHI MINH'S TIME, SEE PAGE 58.

The Vietminh now swarmed into action all over Vietnam. From May onwards Ho Chi Minh was back with the rebels, although he was often ill and suffering from fever. The Americans sent in a unit of troops to help and these were welcomed by Ho Chi Minh.

August 1945

That August, Ho Chi Minh and his fighters heard by radio that **atomic bombs** had been dropped on two Japanese cities. Japan had surrendered to the USA and the most terrible war the world had ever known was over.

In Vietnam, the long years of preparation and planning by Ho Chi Minh and by both Communists and nationalists soon paid off. With amazing speed, Vietminh forces took control of Hanoi, Hué and even Saigon, where Ho Chi Minh's rebels were less well supported than in the north.

Before the French knew it, Bao Dai had given up the throne and the Vietminh were in control of most of the former French **colony**. Independence was declared on 2 September. And the new leader on the platform was none other than Ho Chi Minh, whom, as Nguyen Ai Quoc, the French had been chasing around the world for 26 years.

10 Return of the French

There was one problem with Ho Chi Minh's new Vietnam. The country was still claimed by France. Even though France itself had been invaded and occupied during World War Two, it was still not ready to agree to a free and independent Vietnamese state, especially one led by a **Communist** and an old enemy.

Communists and nationalists

In January 1946 Ho Chi Minh called a general election in all areas under Vietminh control. Many of the **nationalists** who had fought with the Vietminh did not want see a Communist takeover in their country. Against the wishes of many Communists, Ho Chi Minh proposed a **coalition government** (one in which the Communists shared power with the nationalists). It received a big vote of support.

Talks with France

Next, Ho Chi Minh needed to meet the French government. He and other representatives travelled to France for a conference. The talks were delayed because of a change of French government. This gave Ho Chi Minh time to relax at the seaside and meet many ordinary French people. It was almost like a holiday – the first he had ever had. He was well liked by those who met him, who said he was charming, with a good sense of humour.

Talks began at last on 6 July 1946, but the new French government offered very little.

▶ *French Prime Minister Georges Bidault greets Ho Chi Minh before the Paris talks in July 1946.*

TO LOCATE HAIPHONG, SEE THE MAP ON PAGE 6.

Ho Chi Minh did sign an agreement before he returned home, but in fact it was worth nothing. The French had already begun to bomb Haiphong, a major city and port on the Hong River delta.

A new war with France

In 1947 the French started to invade Vietnam all over again. As they re-occupied Hanoi, Ho Chi Minh and his government withdrew and launched a **guerrilla campaign** against them across the countryside. Ho's experience with the Communist troops in China had shown him how effective this kind of fighting could be.

By 1950 France was able to create a new state in the south. This claimed to be an independent nation, although it was firmly under French control. Its new president was the former emperor, Bao Dai. France continued to fight in the north. It was a bitter war.

Key dates: Vietnam's war against France

1945	• Ho Chi Minh declares independence in Hanoi
1946	• January: Vietminh hold general election • July: conference in France on the future of Vietnam
1947	• French troops re-invade Vietnam
1950	• The French set up a new 'independent' state in the south, with Bao Dai as president
1950	• First American military advisers arrive in the southern state
1954	• Defeat of French troops at Dien Bien Phu. The French leave Vietnam for the last time.

A 'Cold War' begins

Ho Chi Minh was still hoping that an international agreement could be reached to bring about peace in Vietnam. However as the war progressed, this seemed less and less likely. The **Cold War** had begun, a long period of political tension between the **capitalist** powers and the Communist countries that now included China, where Mao Zedong had finally defeated the nationalists in 1949.

FOR DETAILS ON KEY PEOPLE OF HO CHI MINH'S TIME, SEE PAGE 58.

The American government believed that **Communism** was the great enemy of **democracy** and that it would spread like wildfire unless it was stopped. They believed that once one country went Communist, then its neighbours would follow. Because Ho Chi Minh was a Communist, the USA saw him as part of this worldwide problem.

Strong roots

'Only when the root is firm can the tree live long,
And victory is built with the people as foundations.'

(Poem by Ho Chi Minh, 1948)

▼ *After 1945 the Indochinese Communist Party divided regionally. Ho Chi Minh formed the Vietnamese Workers' Party (VWP). Here he addresses the VWP National Conference in 1951.*

FOR DETAILS ON KEY PEOPLE OF HO CHI MINH'S TIME, SEE PAGE 58.

Winner takes all

'One of the world's richest areas is open to the winner in Indochina. That's behind the growing US concern ... tin, rubber, rice, key strategic raw materials are what this war is really about.'

(US News and World Report, 4 April 1954)

In fact there were strong disagreements between the Communist countries. The Soviet Union, the world's most powerful Communist country, had by now little interest in foreign **revolutions**, except where they would be of direct benefit to the Russians themselves. In 1950 Ho Chi Minh travelled to Moscow to meet Stalin, but was treated with rudeness and scorn by the Soviet leader who considered him too moderate and too pro-Chinese.

The Americans also wanted to make sure that precious supplies of natural **resources** from South-east Asia, such as tin, **tungsten** and rubber, would not dry up.

Dien Bien Phu

The USA set up a Military and Advisory Group (MAAG) in the southern Vietnamese state and provided 80 per cent of the funding for the French war in the north. They shipped in **napalm** bombs to be dropped by French war planes. By 1954 the French had committed 250,000 troops to the colonial war.

Ho Chi Minh planned war policy carefully with his colleagues, but actual operations were in the hands of his military chief, Vo Nguyen Gap. Their army was provided with food supplies and weapons by the new government in China, but nobody outside Vietnam believed these ragged rebels could defeat the French army.

▶ *A French gun crew at Dien Bien Phu, in March 1954. Just under two months later the French were defeated and about to leave Vietnam for good.*

The great Vietnamese victory came on 7 May 1954, when the French were defeated after eight weeks of fighting at Dien Bien Phu, in the north-western highlands. Ho Chi Minh's supporters, many of them women, had smuggled gun parts through enemy territory and carried them up mountain paths to positions above the French forts. Ten thousand French troops were captured. The defeated French pulled out of Vietnam and the war was suddenly over.

To locate Dien Bien Phu, see the map on page 6.

This battle marked the end of French power in South-east Asia. Ho Chi Minh had seen his dream come true after 35 years. Even so, he knew that the victory was a bitter one. The years of struggle had caused massive loss of life.

You will lose ...

'You can kill ten of my men for every one I kill of yours, but even at those odds I will win and you will lose.'

(Ho Chi Minh, warning the French in 1946)

With the French gone, Ho Chi Minh could now move back into Hanoi and set up the government of the **Democratic Republic of Vietnam (DRV)**. He did this quietly, with little fuss. There were no victory parades.

He moved into a small, simple home in the grounds of a former palace, which had been taken over by the government. Although he was elected president, Ho Chi Minh never approved of the kind of personal hero worship that Stalin encouraged in the Soviet Union. He preferred to see himself as part of a team and never forgot his simple, village origins.

Bao Dai still controlled the south of the country, which was known as the State of Vietnam. Some northerners, opposed to Ho Chi Minh's government, fled south. Many of them were **Roman Catholics**, who feared that they would suffer in the north for following the religion of the old colonial rulers.

▼ *The former emperor Bao Dai (centre, in pale suit) headed the new state in southern Vietnam from 1949 to 1955.*

▲ The Geneva Conference opened immediately after the French defeat of May 1954 and lasted into July. The DRV delegation was led by a **veteran** Vietnamese Communist called Pham Van Dong (front row, third from left).

The Geneva Conference

Ho Chi Minh knew that Vietnam would never find peace without international agreement over its future. It was decided to hold a conference in Geneva, Switzerland. The countries sending representatives were the USA, the Soviet Union, France, Great Britain, China, Cambodia, Laos, the Democratic Republic of Vietnam and the State of Vietnam. Ho Chi Minh did not go to Geneva in person, but when he **briefed** the DRV team, he made it clear that a realistic settlement had to be reached.

The conference concluded that for the time being Vietnam should be divided in two parts, but that elections for a united country should be held no later than 1956. These elections should be supervised internationally to make sure that they were fair. No outside nation was to send troops into Vietnam or offer political backing to either the north or the south.

The USA had no intention of withdrawing its support for the south and did not sign up to the agreement, but it did agree not to challenge it by force. The other countries did sign, although France then declared its support for the south, which of course went against the agreement.

The elections for a united country never happened. Ho Chi Minh called for them to take place year after year, but each time the USA, which was as strongly opposed to **Communism** as ever, claimed that this was just a devious plot by the DRV government. There is little doubt that Ho Chi Minh would have won nationwide elections in the late 1950s.

Land reform

At home, the **Communists** were making enemies, even in the north. Ho Chi Minh was generally seen to be an easy-going character, but many in his party were **hard-liners**.

A programme of land reform was brought in, with the full support of Ho Chi Minh. The aim of the reforms was to give land back to the poorest people in society. Many of the landlords and wealthier farmers who owned most of the land were against these changes. Between 1953 and 1956 the hard-liners followed the example of the Communists in China, using threats, torture and execution to get their way. Ho Chi Minh condemned the violence and **atrocities**, which were eventually halted.

Foreign affairs

Ho Chi Minh was still popular and in 1960 was re-elected president of the Democratic Republic. He spent much of his time working on foreign policy. The international situation was changing fast. Stalin was dead and the Soviet Union had a new leader, Nikita Khrushchev. He was bringing in reforms in the Soviet Union, but tensions with the USA were bringing the world close to **nuclear war**. There was a growing split between China and the Soviet Union, which Ho Chi Minh tried in vain to heal.

How to reunite?

The other question upon which Ho Chi Minh concentrated was **reunification** with the south, where the number of American military advisers was growing rapidly. In 1955 the southern Vietnamese prime minister, Ngo Dinh Diem, brought about the fall of Bao Dai and became president himself after a **rigged election**.

FOR DETAILS ON KEY PEOPLE OF HO CHI MINH'S TIME, SEE PAGE 58.

By 1960 Ho Chi Minh was beginning to think that the southern state might collapse. Ngo Dinh Diem, a Roman Catholic, was very unpopular and had stirred up bitter opposition among non-Catholic religious groups, targeting **Buddhist** monks in particular. Buddhism was the most widely followed religion in Vietnam, while to many **nationalists** Christianity (predominant in the south) was associated with French colonialism.

Communists, too, were persecuted by Ngo Dinh Diem. Faced with jail or execution they started to organize opposition in the south. A local movement called the National Liberation Front was formed. Its fighters called themselves the People's Liberation Armed Force. They became widely known abroad as the Viet Cong (short for *Viet Nam Cong San* or 'Vietnamese Communists'). Ho Chi Minh supported the southern rebels and offered them training.

▶ *Buddhist monks protest against President Ngo Dinh Diem in Saigon, in August 1963.*

12 The Vietnam War

Ho Chi Minh was now in his seventies. His long life of hardship had taken its toll. His health was poor and he looked frail. Younger people were gaining more and more power in the northern government. Many of them wanted to take on the south, but 'Uncle Ho' (as he was known in the north) was still respected and he urged caution.

FOR DETAILS ON KEY PEOPLE OF HO CHI MINH'S TIME, SEE PAGE 58.

He knew that there were more and more American troops in the south, training the southern army. There was growing unrest there, too. In 1963 the unpopular leader Ngo Dinh Diem was overthrown and then murdered by army officers. The new southern leader was a general called Nguyen Cao Ky, who admitted that his personal hero was Germany's **Nazi dictator**, Adolf Hitler.

All-out war

In 1964 two US warships approached the coast of the Gulf of Tonkin, in North Vietnam. They were probably on a spying mission, testing out coastal defences. They were fired upon by the army of the north. This 'Tonkin incident' meant that the USA and the north were now openly at war.

Early in 1965 the Viet Cong attacked an American base in the south. US warplanes started non-stop bombing of the north. Soon there were 200,000 US troops in the south. Later, Australian and New Zealand troops were also sent into what became known as the Vietnam War.

The Vietnam War developed into one of the most brutal conflicts of modern times. **Communist** fighters and weapons passed from north to south down a secret route named the 'Ho Chi Minh Trail'. American planes destroyed cover by stripping vast areas of jungle with leaf-destroying chemicals.

▲ *The US troops were fighting in harsh jungle conditions against a determined enemy.*

American and southern troops set villages ablaze. Their prisoners of war were tortured and thrown from helicopters. Children burned to death with **napalm** sticking to their skins. The Viet Cong too were ruthless fighters and executed many of their opponents, civilian as well as military.

Hero of the protests

Ho Chi Minh was enraged and called upon international leaders to condemn the USA and southern forces. All over the world, young people joined in protests against the war. In Great Britain, France, Germany, the Netherlands, Scandinavia, Italy, Canada, Australia and the USA itself, tens of thousands of demonstrators took to the streets chanting the name of their unlikely new hero – a man old enough to be their grandfather: 'Ho-Ho-Ho, Ho Chi MINH!' It was in this period, when the old rebel was already losing real power at home, that he became most famous around the world. Despite these popular protests, governments tended to side with their **Cold War** positions. Western European countries supported the USA, while Communist countries condemned American actions.

It was the first time ever that the cruel reality of modern warfare had been brought into the home by television news. People in the USA were shocked and public opinion soon became bitterly divided. More and more Americans turned against the war and some refused to serve in the army. However with so many American servicemen being killed in action, other Americans harshly criticized the protestors for being unpatriotic.

Some international protestors made the journey to Vietnam and met Ho Chi Minh for themselves. He enjoyed talking to them. However his health was becoming ever worse. In 1965 he had to go to China for a long rest. Remembering his studies as a schoolboy, he visited the birthplace of the **philosopher** Confucius.

A letter to LBJ

'Vietnam is thousands of miles away from the United States. But contrary to the pledges made by its representative at the 1954 Geneva Conference, the US has ceaselessly intervened in Vietnam ... The Vietnamese people will never submit to force ... Our cause is absolutely just.'

(from a letter sent by Ho Chi Minh to American President Lyndon Baines Johnson, 15 February 1967)

The Tet offensive

By the beginning of 1968, the USA believed that the war was almost won. However for some time Ho Chi Minh and the northern government had been planning a major attack on the south. Ho Chi Minh, in between rest cures, finally ordered this to take place in Tet, the month of the Vietnamese New Year.

About 67,000 combined northern and Viet Cong forces launched a massive attack on all major southern cities. Central Saigon became a battlefield. Thirty aircraft were destroyed at the American airbase at Da Nang. This was no victory for the Communists, for they suffered very heavy losses. However it shocked the southern and American governments beyond belief. They had not believed that such an attack was even possible. The American public began to wonder if the war really was going as well for the USA as had been claimed. In revenge for the **offensive**, US aircraft destroyed the city of Hué with bombs – but many Americans were beginning to wonder if this terrible war could ever be won.

Ho Chi Minh, the **veteran** of so many wars, sensed at once that the 'Tet offensive' marked a turning point. He felt like a younger man. He even tried to persuade his colleagues that he should travel secretly into the south, just as he had crossed over to Pac Bo during World War Two. He wanted to inspire the men and women who were fighting, but he was now too frail to attempt such a mission.

▼ *Dressed in a cap and scarf, wearing spectacles, 78-year-old Ho Chi Minh addresses villagers during a tour of northern Vietnam.*

13 An old man dies

Bombs were falling on Hanoi, but Ho Chi Minh tried to find peace in his old age. He was still in his simple home, looking after his garden, feeding the goldfish in the pond. He received official visitors and he advised the northern government on policy, but he was no longer involved in everyday affairs.

War or peace?

In March 1968 the American president, Lyndon Baines Johnson, weary of battling with public opinion at home, announced that he would resign from politics at the following election.

FOR DETAILS ON KEY PEOPLE OF HO CHI MINH'S TIME, SEE PAGE 58.

That May, the USA and the government of North Vietnam at last agreed to meet and talk about peace. A conference began in Paris. Ho Chi Minh's advice to his government was to be wary, but to work towards a settlement. However at the conference table, neither side was able to make progress. The talks would drag on for four more years, getting nowhere.

Johnson's successor in the November election was Richard Nixon, who had been a fierce critic of **Communism** since the start of the **Cold War**. Nixon reduced the number of troops in Vietnam, but stepped up the bombing. He extended it to areas of neighbouring Cambodia, where there had been support for the northern and Viet Cong forces since 1965. By April 1969 more than 33,000 American soldiers had been killed in Vietnam. In North America and Europe protests against the war were becoming ever louder. The war seemed to have run out of control.

The last summer

On 19 May 1969 Ho Chi Minh celebrated his 79th birthday. His friends encouraged him, telling him that he would live to see victory. However during that long, hot summer, his health became very much worse. He had chest pains and heart trouble. On the morning of 2 September 1969, after drinking some rice water, 'Uncle Ho' had a sudden heart attack and died.

The death of Ho Chi Minh was announced by Radio Hanoi on 3 September. The Viet Cong forces in the south declared a three-day truce in his memory. World leaders paid tribute to him, including many who were not **Communists**. The USA and its **allies** did not praise their old enemy, but some did admit that the charming, witty Ho Chi Minh might have been easier to talk to than the new generation of leaders in North Vietnam.

▶ *In 1969 Ho Chi Minh was still full of spirit and humour, but physically he was very frail.*

The funeral

About 100,000 people came to the state funeral for Ho Chi Minh, six days after his death. It was held in Da Binh square, Hanoi, where he had declared Vietnamese independence in September 1945.

Ho had often stated that he wanted a simple **cremation** when he died. It would be healthier that way, he had said, and save good land for farming! However the government ordered his body to be **embalmed** instead and seven years later it was placed inside a grand **mausoleum** overlooking Da Binh square. Vietnam's rulers wanted a glorious monument. The old man would not have approved.

▶ *Ho Chi Minh's admirers visit the mausoleum on Vietnam's National Day, 2 September. This date commemorates both the Vietnamese Declaration of Independence in 1945 and Ho Chi Minh's death in 1969.*

14 The world after Ho

Ho Chi Minh did not live to see Vietnam reunited. However he was right to have seen the Tet **offensive** as a turning point in the Vietnam War.

In March 1972 units of the North Vietnamese army, numbering 120,000 men, invaded the south with the help of local Viet Cong. There was more massive American bombing of the north, but by 1973 President Nixon and his adviser Henry Kissinger had realized that this war could not be won. The USA declared a ceasefire on 27 January 1973. Nixon called it 'peace with honour', but to many Americans it seemed more like a defeat.

Ho Chi Minh City

South Vietnam fought on against the north in what was now a **civil war**. On 30 April 1975 it surrendered to the north. There were desperate scenes as Americans fled the US embassy in Saigon by helicopter. Thousands of their Vietnamese supporters tried to escape with them.

The fall of Saigon brought to an end the struggle that Ho Chi Minh had started before World War One. The capital city of the south, from which Ho Chi Minh had started his journey to Europe in 1911, was officially renamed in his honour: Ho Chi Minh City.

A new nation

Vietnam was now a single country with a **Communist** government. However old divisions were not healed. The Communist government was disliked by many **nationalists**, and there was still tension between the mainly Communist north and the mainly nationalist south.

Many Vietnamese fled the country in search of a better economic life, some of them escaping to Hong Kong and other Asian ports in leaky boats. Communities of Vietnamese **exiles** grew up in the USA, Canada, Australia and many other parts of the world.

The world moves on

However over the years, the world changed. The Soviet Union collapsed in 1990, bringing an end to the **Cold War**. The Chinese government brought in **capitalist** reforms, although it still claimed to be following Communist policies. Vietnam too brought in reforms, made its peace with the United States and opened up to international trade. By the 1990s Western tourists were pouring into Vietnam and Da Nang was famous not for its airbase but for its seaside surfers. This turned out to be the new world for which Ho Chi Minh laid the foundations.

▼ *Crowds and traffic throng the streets of Saigon, now officially known as Ho Chi Minh City.*

Man of mystery

Although Ho Chi Minh was present at many of the great events of the last century, he remains something of a man of mystery. Perhaps this is because for much of his life he was trying to keep hidden, changing his name, and travelling in disguise. He had at least one marriage and several girlfriends, but no family life. Politics was his world, but it is hard to find the private person beneath the public figure.

When we look back at Ho Chi Minh's life, we see all sorts of contradictions. He was a Communist who spent much of his life arguing with other Communists. He fought the French and yet spent some of his happiest days in France and was a lover of the French language. He was an admirer of the United States and yet he became its greatest enemy.

Ho Chi Minh met many of the most important people of his day, but he himself lived in the simplest way possible, without riches, fine houses or expensive clothes. He spent much of his life at war, and yet he longed for peace.

To many people in Vietnam and in other parts of the world, Ho Chi Minh is still a figure to be admired, a fighter for freedom. Many thousands died in the Vietnam War, and Ho Chi Minh must bear some responsibility. However he was not some power-mad **dictator**. Most people who met him during his life, including some of his political enemies, found him to be a likeable, friendly man.

The man who never gave up

He was of course single-minded, for he was driven forward by his politics for 50 years. Any one of his **campaigns** would have been enough to exhaust most ordinary people, but he carried on and on – and on. One reason Ho Chi Minh

▲ *Italian anti-war protestors carry pictures of Ho Chi Minh through the streets of Rome in 1967. His political ideas influenced a generation.*

survived so long was his political cunning. He was always cautious, never in a hurry. He knew when to talk and make a **compromise**, and when to press forward with action. He was a realist, a natural 'wheeler and dealer'.

From 1919 onwards Ho Chi Minh attempted time after time after time to achieve a just settlement for his country through international **negotiation**. It is probably true to say that the bloodshed of the French and American wars in Vietnam could have been prevented if the Western countries had been prepared to come to an agreement with Ho Chi Minh. They had the chance in 1919, in 1945, in the later 1950s, and in 1964, but each time they ignored him it cost them dearly. The cost to the people of Vietnam of both the Communist and nationalist struggles was also very high. The Tet offensive alone caused massive loss of life.

A lifetime's struggle

'Without the cold and desolation of winter,
There could not be the warmth and splendour of spring:
Calamity has tempered and hardened me
And turned my mind into steel.'

(Poem by Ho Chi Minh)

A place in history

It is sometimes said that people shape history. Ho Chi Minh would have disagreed. He would have declared that history was not made by individual people, but by whole classes of people as they react to the economic conditions under which they live.

Ho Chi Minh did not create the events that shook the world in his day, but he certainly took them on and faced up to them. Even those who disagree with his politics agree that in his struggle to change society, Ho Chi Minh was a tireless fighter and a remarkable man.

▶ *A statue of Ho Chi Minh looks across the city that now bears his name.*

Timeline

1890	Ho Chi Minh is born.
1901	Death of Ho's mother. Ho Chi Minh comes of age.
1907	Ho Chi Minh attends the National Academy in Hué.
1908	Ho's support for protesting farmers leads to his expulsion from the academy.
1911–17	Ho Chi Minh travels round the world. Works in the USA and in London, England.
1917	Ho Chi Minh finds work in Paris.
1919	Ho Chi Minh and friends form the Society of Annamese Patriots in Paris. Ho Chi Minh adopts the name Nguyen Ai Quoc.
1923	Ho Chi Minh sails to the Soviet Union, works for the Comintern and studies Communist theory.
1924	Ho Chi Minh travels to Guangzhou, China, to make contact with Communist revolutionaries.
1927	Vietnamese nationalists found the Viet Quoc. Ho Chi Minh marries Tang Tuyet Minh. The Chinese nationalist leader Jiang Jieshi captures Shanghai and Guangzhou. Ho Chi Minh flees to Hong Kong.
1927–30	Ho Chi Minh travels to the Soviet Union, Germany, France, Italy, and Siam as a secret agent for the Comintern.
1930	Ho Chi Minh returns to Hong Kong, where he forms the united Vietnamese Communist Party.
1931–32	Uprisings by both Communists and nationalists in Vietnam. Ho Chi Minh imprisoned in Hong Kong.
1934	Ho Chi Minh returns to Moscow.
1938	Ho Chi Minh returns to China from Moscow, working in Guilin as a journalist and health officer.
1939	Ho Chi Minh travels around China for the Comintern.
1940	Japanese troops enter Vietnam.

1941	Vietminh forces are founded to fight the French and Japanese in Vietnam. Ho Chi Minh returns secretly to Vietnam.
1942	Ho Chi Minh returns to China where he is imprisoned on suspicion of spying for the Japanese.
1944	Ho Chi Minh regains freedom. Returns to Vietnam.
1945	Vietminh campaign all over Vietnam. Japan defeated. Vietminh forces control most of Vietnam. Ho Chi Minh declares independence in Hanoi.
1946	Vietminh hold general election. Coalition government wins support. Ho Chi Minh travels to France for conference on the future of Vietnam.
1947	French troops re-invade Vietnam.
1950	The French set up a new 'independent' state in the south, with Bao Dai as president.
1954	Defeat of French troops at Dien Bien Phu. The French leave Vietnam.
1953–56	Land reforms brought in by Ho Chi Minh in the north bring cruelty and violence, which is condemned by Ho Chi Minh.
1954	Conference in Geneva, Switzerland, agrees elections for a united Vietnam will be held by 1956.
1955	Bao Dai forced from power in South Vietnam.
1956–60	South Vietnam and USA reject Ho Chi Minh's calls for joint elections as agreed in Geneva.
1960	Founding of NLF and Viet Cong in South Vietnam.
1963	USA sends troops to South Vietnam. South Vietnamese government is overthrown by the army.
1964	North Vietnam engages American navy. USA starts bombing North Vietnam and sends in marines.
1965	Start of worldwide opposition to Vietnam War. Ho Chi Minh is the protestors' hero.
1968	Tet offensive against South Vietnam and US forces.
1969	Death of Ho Chi Minh.

Key people of Ho Chi Minh's time

Bao Dai (1913–97). Bao Dai was the son of the emperor Khai Dai and came to the throne himself in 1932, although real power remained with the French colonial government. He was forced from rule by Ho Chi Minh in 1945, who kept him on as an adviser to the Vietminh government. However he fled, only to return as president of the new French-backed southern Vietnamese state in 1949. He was forced from office by Ngo Diem Dinh in 1955, and lived in exile in France.

Jiang Jieshi (1887–1975). Jiang Jieshi (Chiang Kai-shek) was the Chinese general who fought to reunite his country for the **nationalist** Guomindang. He became party leader, ordering an attack on his **Communist allies**. He joined up with them again in order to fight the Japanese invasion, but in 1948 was forced from the mainland by the Communists. He set up a rival Chinese state on the island of Taiwan.

Johnson, Lyndon Baines (1908–73). 'LBJ' was a politician with a strong interest in **social justice**. He became president upon the assassination of John F Kennedy in 1963. While 'JFK' had stepped up the US presence in Vietnam, under 'LBJ' it grew rapidly. As the war became ever more unpopular, Johnson drew much of the blame. He once said that if he and Ho Chi Minh could ever get together, they could probably sort out their differences one-to-one. He retired in 1968.

Lenin, Vladimir Ilyich (1870–1924). Lenin was a brilliant thinker and and a shrewd politician who became a Communist activist and played the key role in the Russian **revolution** of November 1917. Lenin saw the new Communist state through a bitter **civil war** and economic hardship.

Mao Zedong (1893–1976). Mao Zedong (Mao Tse-Tung) founded the Chinese Communist Party in 1921 and led a brilliant **guerrilla campaign** against both the Japanese and the nationalists. Mao provided the North Vietnamese with aid in their war with the USA.

Ngo Dinh Diem (1901–63). A devout **Roman Catholic**, Ngo Dinh Diem became a successful government minister during the colonial period. In 1950 he left Vietnam, refusing to support either Ho Chi Minh or Bao Dai. With US support, he returned to South Vietnam as prime minister in 1954 and the following year became president. He was unpopular and corrupt and a persecutor of **Buddhists**. He was overthrown with the agreement of the USA in 1963 and was then murdered.

Nguyen Cao Ky (1930–). Having fought with the French against the Vietminh, Ky became an airforce commander in South Vietnam and then president in 1965. He retired in 1971 and left Vietnam for the USA in 1975.

Stalin, Joseph (1879–1953). Stalin took part in the Russian revolution of November 1917, in which the Communists overthrew the government. He gained power in the Soviet Union after 1924. Stalin was a ruthless leader, who pushed through reforms even when they caused extreme hardship. Many of his opponents were exiled, imprisoned or murdered. He was a cunning international politician and played an important part in the Allied victory in World War Two.

Vo Nguyen Giap (1912–). When Vo Nguyen Giap was a history teacher in Vietnam, he studied the military tactics of Napoleon, the French leader in the early 1800s. When the Vietminh was formed, it was he who became their military chief. He built up the small guerrilla force into an extremely effective army, which in 1954 defeated the French at Dien Bien Phu. He commanded the northern army during the Vietnam War of the 1960s.

Further reading & other resources

Further reading
The Fall of Saigon: The End of the Vietnam War, Michael V Uschan, Heinemann Library, 2002

History for GCSE: Vietnam, Philip Sauvain, Nelson Thomas, 1997

Ho, David Halberstam, McGraw Hill College, 1986

The USA and Vietnam, Vivienne Saunders, Hodder and Stoughton Educational, 2002

Sources
Ho Chi Minh: A Life, William J Duiker, Hyperion, 2000

Websites
http://www.time.com/time/time100/leaders/profile/hochiminh.html

http://www.fordham.edu/halsall/mod/1930hochiminh/

http://www.moreorless.au.com/heroes/ho

http:/www.dir.yahoo.com/Arts/Humanities/By_Time_Period/20th_Century/Military/History/Vietnam

http://www.pbs.org.wbh/amex/vietnam/

http://servercc.oakton.edu/~wittmann/

Glossary

allies countries (or people) who are on the same side and support each other in a conflict

atomic bomb a bomb in which a nuclear reaction takes place, creating a massive explosion

atrocities cruel or violent deeds

brief to pass on to someone a plan of action or information

Buddhist follower of a religion of eastern and central Asia based on the teaching of Gautama Buddha

campaign a programme of activities or military action, with a particular purpose

capitalism economic system based on private ownership of industry and resources

capitalist describes the economic system based on private ownership of industry and resources

civil war war fought between rival groups in the same country

coalition government government that is made up of an alliance between different political parties

Cold War long period of political tension (1945–90) between the USA, and its allies, and the Communist countries, which included the Soviet Union and China

colonies countries ruled by another country

Comintern Communist International, an international workers' association founded in 1919

Communism political and economic system in which all property is owned by everyone

Communist someone who belongs to or believing in a political and economic system in which all property is owned by everyone

compromise deal with or make concessions to an opponent to reach a settlement

cremation burning of a dead body

democracy government by the majority of the people or their elected representatives

democratic describing government by the majority of the people or their elected representatives

deport remove someone from a country

detain to hold someone and prevent their free movement

dictator someone who governs with absolute authority

embalm to preserve a dead body with chemicals

exile someone who has been officially banned from their homeland

famine period of widespread and extreme hunger

Great Depression time of widespread business failures and job losses in the USA that began in 1929 and continued through the 1930s

guerrilla describes a band of irregular fighters who harass the enemy with small attacks and ambushes

hard-liner someone who refuses to compromise or change their policy

human right claim to be treated according to values which are common to humanity, such as freedom from slavery

lobby to meet politicans or others in order to persuade them to do something

mausoleum tomb which is built as a grand monument

napalm flaming petroleum jelly used in bombs and flame-throwers, causing severe injuries to victims

nationalist someone (or description of someone) who believes that a country has the right to rule itself. In the struggles for self-rule in Vietnam and China the term refers to nationalists who were opposed to Communism.

Nazi member of (or describing) the German National Socialist Workers' Party, a racist, violent and anti-democratic political group, which ruled Germany from 1933–45

negotiation discussions to reach an agreed settlement

nuclear war warfare in which nuclear weapons of mass destruction are used

offensive attacking phase of a military campaign

patriot someone who loves their country

peace treaty the terms of settlement at the end of a war

philosopher someone who studies ideas and behaviour

plantation large estate given over to the growing of certain crops, such as rubber or sugar cane

resources country's wealth in the form of useful minerals, timber, water, etc

reunification making a divided country into a single nation again

revolution complete change in the way that society is run. It may be brought about by the overthrow of a government.

revolutionary someone who calls for a revolution, or takes part in one

rigged election election in which the result is produced dishonestly

Roman Catholic belonging to the Christian group which is headed by the Pope in Rome

share one of the units into which a company's wealth is divided in order to be bought and sold by the public

socialist somebody who supports public ownership and regulation of the economy in the interests of all

social justice the principle of fairness and equality

spiritual concerned with the world of the spirit, rather than the world of material things

striking refusing to work until grievances have been met

tuberculosis infectious disease which affects the lungs

tungsten rare and valuable metal used in the manufacture of steel machine tools and lamp filaments

veteran someone who is very experienced

warlord leader who uses military force to control a region of a country, opposing the authority of central government

working class group of people in society who earn wages by labouring or making things

Index

Association of Annamese Patriots 14–15

Bao Dai 34, 36, 40, 43
Bidault, Georges 35
Buddhism 43

China
    Ho Chi Minh in 20–22, 25, 28, 31, 46
    Japanese invasion of 28
Cold War 5, 37, 52
Comintern 17, 18, 20, 21, 23, 28, 29
Confucius 9, 46

Da Nang 47, 52
Declaration of Independence, Vietnamese
    4, 5, 34
Dien Bien Phu 39

France
    Ho Chi Minh in 11, 12, 13–17, 22, 35
    rule in Vietnam 6, 7–8, 10, 29, 35–39
French Indochina 6

Gandhi, Mohandas Karamchand 26–27
Geneva Conference 41
Great Depression 22, 24
Guangzhou (Canton) 20–22
Guilin 28–29

Haiphong 36
Hanoi 4, 34, 36, 48, 50
Ho Chi Minh
    birth and education 6–10
    death 48–50
    in China 20–22, 25, 28, 31, 46
    in England 13
    in France 11, 12, 13–17, 22, 35
    in Siam 22, 23
    in the Soviet Union 18–20, 22, 25–26,
    38
    in the USA 12
    political beliefs 8, 13–15, 16–17, 19
    president of DRV 40, 42
Ho Chi Minh City 51, 52
Hoang Thi Loan 6
Hoang Tru 6, 7
Hong Kong 22, 23, 24–25, 52
Hué 6–7, 9–10, 34, 47

Japan
    invasion of China 28
    invasion of Vietnam 29–30, 34
Jiang Jieshi (Chiang Kai-Shek) 18, 21–22
Johnson, Lyndon Baines 48

Khrushchev, Nikita 42
Kim Lien 7
Kissinger, Henry 51
Kunming 33

London 13

Moscow 18–19, 22, 25, 38

New York City 12
Ngo Dinh Diem 43, 44
Nguyen Ai Quoc 14, 15
Nguyen Cao Ky 44
Nguyen Sinh Cung 6
Nguyen Sinh Sac 7–8, 9, 10
Nguyen Tat Thanh 9
Nguyen Thi Minh Kai 25
Nixon, Richard 48, 51

Pac Bo 31, 33
Paris 13, 14–15, 48
Pham Van Dong 41

Saigon 10, 11, 34, 43, 47, 51, 52
Shanghai 21, 22, 25
Stalin, Joseph 25–26, 29, 38, 42
Sun Zhongsgang (Sun Yat-sen) 18

Tang Tuyet Minh 21
Tours, conference at 16–17

USA
    Ho Chi Minh in 12
    involvement in Vietnam 33, 37, 38, 41,
    42, 44–48, 51, 52

Van Ba 11
Viet Cong 43, 44, 45, 47, 49, 51
Viet Quoc 23
Vietminh 31–32, 33, 34, 35
Vietnam
    Democratic Republic of (DRV) 40, 41
    French rule in 6, 7–8, 10, 29, 35–39
    Japanese invasion of 29–30, 34
    State of 40, 41
    US involvement in 33, 37, 38, 41, 42,
    44–48, 51, 52
Vietnam War 44–48, 51
Vinh 9
Vo Nguyen Gap 38
Vuong Thuc Qui 9

World War One 5, 13
World War Two 5, 29–34

Zhou Enlai (Chou En-Lai) 19